WHAT'S BEHIND THE EXCUSES

FINANCIALLY SPEAKING

KIM ANGELA LEE

What's Behind The Excuses

Excuses

Financially Speaking

Kim Angela Lee

Published by
"Nickels and Dimes Solutions, L.L.C."

Printed in the United States of America

This book has been edited by Leteisha Tate
royalimagecoachingconsulting@gmail.com

ISBN: 9798883445223
Copyright: Int CI-3875706113 @2024

Dedication

This dedication is for those who have believed in me and trusted me to assist them on their journey.

Thank you to those who recognized the stories within me.

It is also dedicated to everyone who has contributed to the success of this book.

Encouraged me to pursue my dreams and helped me achieve the

Table of Contents

Introduction 6

Chapter 1: Unraveling the Deception Within

Our Finances 8

Chapter 2: Unpacking Financial Commitments -

What's Behind the Hesitation 17

Chapter 3: Restlessness and Your Financial

Journey 25

Chapter 4: The Hidden Masks of

Financial Deception 33

Chapter 5: Trust and Confidences –

Navigating Financial Challenges............ 40

Chapter 6: Correcting Misconceptions

About Money 46

Meet the Author 53

Introduction

In the opening pages of my book, I delve into the many excuses people make about money when faced with the idea of making and sticking to an excellent financial plan.

Drawing from my client experiences, a recurring theme becomes visible; a resistance to committing to decisive financial practices, such as budgeting.

As I navigate through the stories of my clients and dissect the various excuses they present for avoiding a simplistic financial plan, a thought-provoking question surfaces:

Why do people selectively pick and choose certain aspects of financial planning while neglecting others?

Remarkably, my findings suggest that the root cause extends beyond the mere surface of monetary concerns.

While the surface-level reasons may manifest as financial constraints, a closer examination reveals that, in most cases, it's not truly about the money. Instead, underlying issues come to the forefront, weaving a complex tapestry of emotions, beliefs, past experiences, and psychological factors that shape individuals' attitudes and behaviors toward their finances.

In the following pages, I unravel the layers of these underlying issues, offering readers a profound exploration into the psychological landscape of financial decision-making.

By shining a light on the deeper aspects influencing individuals' choices, my aim is to provide not only an understanding of the complexities surrounding financial excuses but also practical strategies to address and overcome these challenges.

Join me on this enlightening journey as we uncover the hidden forces that shape our financial behaviors and discover a path toward building a more secure and fulfilling financial future.

1

Chapter 1: Unraveling the Root of Deception within Your Financial Decisions

In this chapter, I will examine the underlying motivations that drive our monetary attitudes and behaviors that lead us to self-deception when handling our finances.

When it comes to money behaviors, there are several underlying behaviors and actions that drive individuals to spend money in a certain way. Let's take a closer look at some of the most common spending habits:

Some people tend to spend money as soon as they get it. This behavior is driven by the desire for instant self-gratification and the need to fulfill immediate wants and desires.

Others tend to hoard money due to a poverty mentality that provokes fear of lack. This behavior is driven by a deep-seated belief that there will not be enough money to take care of things that will arise in the future.

Savers tend to save money as a way to create a sense of stability and security. This behavior is driven by the need to feel financially secure and prepared for any unexpected events that may arise.

On the other hand, some choose to invest, and investors tend to focus on making investments that will provide them with long-term benefits for the future. This behavior is driven by the desire to secure a comfortable future for themselves and their loved ones.

For some, money is a symbol of social status and pride, so they tend to spend money to give others an appearance of their wealth and status.

This behavior is called "Keeping up with the Joneses," and is driven by the need to be perceived as successful and have a high reputation.

It is important to note that these behaviors are not mutually exclusive, and individuals may combine these behaviors. Taking the time to understand yourself and your underlying behavior behind spending money and the habits that follow can help individuals make informed decisions about their finances and develop better money habits and practices.

It's time to take a look at this sneaky behavior.
Self-deception, at its core, involves the act of misleading oneself or accepting a distorted version or facade when it concerns our true nature, attitude, emotions, and values regarding money. As we navigate life, much of what we've learned about money connects us to the false narratives and self-deception that create belief systems around the reasons we need to spend money.

The phenomenon around our money stories influences a spectrum of facets in our lives that range from materialism to ethical considerations.

Money has multifaceted forms that manipulate a remarkable influence over our existence. It can serve as a tool to satisfy fundamental needs,

provide security, and furnish opportunities for personal development and enjoyment.

Nevertheless, it can also disguise its use as a wellspring of self-deception, blinding our core values and leading us down a path that detours us from our authentic selves.

In today's world of glitz, glam, and materialism, there is a relentless pursuit of our hard-earned money. The overwhelming influx of spending temptations is hard to escape, with so many of our desires seeking to lay claim to our resources.

One of the most prevalent ways money fosters self-deception is through materialism. The consistent pursuit of material possessions can lead individuals to overestimate their self-worth based on their possessions. They may equate the size of their bank balance with their own projected value, mistakenly believing that accumulating more material possessions will undoubtedly bring them happiness.

In all truth, genuine happiness often derives from good experiences, relationships, and personal internal fulfillment rather than accumulating possessions.

Within this realm of self-deception, individuals risk losing sight of their authentic values.

Pursuing money and material goods consumes them to the point where they neglect their passions, relationships, and overall well-being. Recognizing when you are ensnared by this self-deceptive trap is imperative for you to reassess your priorities.

Another trick of money-related self-deception pertains to an individual's perception of financial risk. Some may deceive themselves about their tolerance for risk when it's time to make investments and financial decisions, downplaying their concerns to justify potentially bad choices.

This can result in reckless financial spending and investments in things that undermine their financial stability.

Understanding your capacity for risk is vital for making informed financial decisions. Deception in this context can yield extreme consequences.

It is crucial to be candid about financial risks and take measures to mitigate them rather than relying on self-deception as a false sense of security.

Money can also be a catalyst for self-deception regarding status and image. The pursuit of wealth and possessions often carries with it the allure of success and a facade of social standing. People may employ their financial accomplishments to deceive themselves and others about their life status, prioritizing appearances over authenticity. This can lead you into an endless cycle of maintaining an image disconnected from your core values and emotions.

In such a scenario, you can find yourself trapped, unable to break free from an ongoing charade inconsistent with your authentic nature.

Authenticity and self-acceptance are pivotal in achieving lasting contentment and satisfaction.

The pursuit of wealth can sometimes result in emotional suppression. Individuals may persuade themselves that they are untroubled by extended working hours or the ethical implications of their actions when, in reality, they are suppressing their true emotions and ethical values. This suppression can lead to dissatisfaction, burnout, and a sense of disconnection from their true selves.

It is vital to recognize when this self-deception takes hold and to take steps to confront it. Honest self-reflection can empower you to unveil your genuine emotions and values, aligning your actions with your true self.

When one is on a continuous quest for wealth, you may mislead yourself into believing that you are making necessary sacrifices for a brighter future.

However, these sacrifices may have a hefty toll, prioritizing financial gain over personal relationships, health, and well-being. This can lead to a lopsided existence devoid of the meaningful connections and experiences that genuinely enrich our lives.

For individuals, achieving a balance between financial aspirations and personal lives is imperative. Recognizing the potential for self-deception in this domain is a step toward unraveling the deception with your finances.

Arguably, the most disheartening facet of self-deception concerning money is rationalizing unethical behavior.

The pursuit of wealth entices individuals to engage in actions that conflict with their moral values. Self-deception may lead them to rationalize these actions, convincing themselves that their behavior is excusable in the name of financial gain.

This brand of self-deception can have far-reaching consequences, affecting an individual's personal integrity and how they navigate society as a whole. It is paramount for individuals to remain vigilant and uphold their ethical standards, even when confronted with financial enticements.

The quest for money can sometimes obscure our judgment and foster self-deception in various aspects of life. Individuals must engage in periodic self-reflection, scrutinize their behaviors, and ensure that their financial pursuits align with their true nature, values, and emotions rather than being solely driven by the allure of monetary wealth

2

Chapter 2: Unpacking the Emotions in Making Financial Commitments - What's Behind the Hesitation

Financial commitments play a major role in shaping our financial futures, yet many individuals grapple with hesitation when committing their finances when moving forward, financially speaking.

In this chapter, we will delve into the underlying reasons why people often find themselves reluctant to make financial commitments.

When it comes to financial matters, individuals often find themselves grappling with an influx of emotions and uncertainties, leading to hesitation, wavering, vacillation, and faltering in decision-making.

The complex nature of making financial choices and the inherent risks can evoke a sense of unease and indecision.

Hesitation may stem from the fear of making the wrong investment or the uncertainty surrounding economic fluctuations.

Wavering could result from conflicting advice or external factors influencing one's financial state of mind.

Indecision might arise from constantly evaluating multiple options, each with its own pros and cons.

Faltering may occur when faced with unexpected challenges or market unpredictability, causing a momentary setback in having financial confidence when making decisions.

In navigating the detailed landscape of finances, individuals often grapple with several types of emotions, shaping how they approach and make decisions in money management.

One common factor that deters individuals from financial commitments is taking risks. The fear of losing money can be a significant barrier to committing to investments or ventures with high financial risk. For instance, someone may be hesitant to invest in stocks because they fear the unpredictability of the stock market and the potential for financial loss.

Financial constraints, such as limited disposable income or savings, can restrict individuals from making financial commitments. Suppose someone's budget is already stretched to its limits. In that case, they may be unable to commit to various financial endeavors, such as retirement savings, because they simply don't have the funds available.

Trust is a fundamental aspect of any financial commitment. Individuals may hesitate due to previous negative experiences, whether with financial institutions, investment decisions, or even personal relationships. Building trust involves transparent communication, reliable financial advice, and understanding the consequences of financial decisions.

Emotional Factors:
Emotions play a significant role in financial decisions. Fear, anxiety, greed, and uncertainty can hinder one's ability to commit to financial plans.

Recognizing and managing emotions is crucial for making sound financial choices. This involves understanding the emotional impact of financial decisions and finding ways to navigate them effectively.

Lack of Clear Goals:
Individuals may struggle to commit to a specific financial path without clear financial goals. Establishing short-term and long-term objectives provides direction and motivation. Whether saving for a home, retirement, or education,

having clear goals helps make informed financial commitments. Setting clear and achievable financial goals provides direction and motivation.

Economic Conditions:
External factors, such as economic conditions, can influence financial commitments. Economic uncertainties, recessions, or inflation can create hesitation. Understanding the broader economic landscape and adapting financial strategies accordingly is essential for navigating through changing conditions.

Peer Pressure:
Social influences and peer pressure can impact financial decisions. People may feel compelled to match the spending habits of their peers, leading to financial commitments that are not aligned with their own needs and goals. Developing financial confidence and independence is crucial in resisting peer pressure.

Peer Influence:
While it's important to consider peer opinions, financial decisions should ultimately align with individual financial goals and values. It's crucial to avoid making commitments solely to conform

to peer pressure.

Education:
A lack of financial literacy can contribute to hesitation in making commitments. Education plays a vital role in empowering individuals to make informed financial decisions. Improving financial literacy through workshops, courses, and self-education can boost confidence and clarity.

Emotional Awareness:
Being aware of the emotional factors that influence financial decisions can enable individuals to make more rational choices and avoid impulsive decisions.

Clear Financial Goals:
Having a clear vision of financial goals is a powerful motivator. Whether creating an emergency fund, paying off debt, or investing for the future, defining specific and achievable goals helps make committed financial decisions.

Financial Planning:
A structured financial plan is key to successful commitments. This involves budgeting, saving, investing, and managing debt. Working with financial professionals or using tools to create a personalized financial plan can provide guidance and increase confidence in financial commitments.

By addressing these factors, individuals can better understand the underlying reasons for hesitation and work towards building a solid foundation for their financial commitments. Understanding these psychological, emotional, and practical barriers can help develop strategies and solutions to move you from hesitation to motivation.

In conclusion, financial commitments are pivotal in achieving financial goals and securing one's financial future. However, various factors can lead to hesitation when it comes to committing funds.

By addressing these concerns, gaining financial knowledge, setting clear goals, and seeking professional advice, individuals can make more confident and informed financial commitments that align with their unique financial circumstances and aspirations.

3

Chapter 3: Overcoming the Restlessness in Your Financial Journey

Restlessness is a common and often unsettling emotion when managing one's finances. The fear of not having enough money or making unwise financial decisions can be overwhelming, leading to impulsive financial behaviors.

In this chapter, we will explore the restlessness that can invade your financial life, identify the underlying causes, and provide strategies to overcome this anxiety and regain control over your financial well-being.

Restlessness concerning your finances can manifest in various ways. For some, it may trigger overspending when boredom strikes, and for others, it can lead to a constant worry about the condition of their finances. Understanding the root causes of this restlessness and learning to manage it is essential for maintaining financial stability and peace of mind.

Boredom and Overspending: What's Behind It?

One common manifestation of financial restlessness is overspending driven by boredom. Many individuals find themselves reaching for their wallets or credit cards when they have idle time or are simply bored. What's really behind this behavior?

Boredom spending can be a coping mechanism to fill a void or seek momentary excitement.
Retail therapy, for instance, is a term used to describe the act of shopping to boost one's mood or alleviate boredom. It often provides a short-lived sense of pleasure or distraction from life's

challenges. People can experience restlessness with their financial journey for various reasons. Common factors contributing to this feeling may be an uncertain future, mounting debt, inadequate savings, comparison, etc.

The future is unpredictable, which can cause anxiety regarding financial security.

Economic conditions, job situation, and global events are all factors that can impact your financial situation. In the midst of a sea of information, opinions, and conflicting advice, navigating the financial landscape can be challenging. Determining fact from fiction is key to making informed financial decisions.

Accumulating debt, whether from student loans, credit cards, or other sources, can be overwhelming and lead to financial restlessness. Dumping debt and working on savings at the same time can be a juggle when trying to create balance. On the other hand, insufficient savings for emergencies or long-term goals may cause individuals to feel unprepared and uneasy about their financial well-being.

Yes, we are still talking about restlessness -financially speaking. A lack of understanding about personal finance, investments, and financial planning can lead to poor decision-making and contribute to restlessness.

Constantly comparing one's financial situation to others, especially in the age of social media, can foster feelings of inadequacy and restlessness.

Succumbing to overspending habits without a clear budget or financial plan can lead to regret and dissatisfaction with one's financial choices.

Continuous buying is often associated with a range of emotions, such as excitement, desire, overspending, and sometimes regret. It can be driven by various factors, including the desire for instant gratification, emotional triggers, or the influence of marketing and advertising. The emotional aspect of impulsive buying can vary from person to person, and individuals may experience a mix of positive and negative emotions during and after the impulsive buying behavior. It's time to do a self-check to see if you fit into the overspending category.

In this context, understanding the psychology behind boredom spending is crucial. The pleasure derived from acquiring new possessions or indulging in temporary experiences can be enticing. However, it often leads to financial regret once the initial excitement disappears.

Tips to Manage Restlessness and Financial Anxiety:

Create a Budget:
Begin your journey to financial peace by creating a budget. Start by tracking your income and expenses to clearly understand your financial situation. A budget helps you see where your money is going and identify areas where you can cut back. By assigning your income into different categories, you'll gain control over your finances and reduce restlessness stemming from financial uncertainty.

Set Financial Goals:

Establishing clear financial goals is an effective way to stay motivated and focused. Whether saving for a down payment on a house, paying off debt, or planning a dream vacation, having specific financial objectives provides a sense of purpose and direction. These goals act as a roadmap to guide your financial decisions and curb restlessness.

Build an Emergency Fund:

One of the primary sources of financial restlessness is the fear of unexpected expenses. Building an emergency fund can offer peace of mind and financial security. This fund is a safety net to cover unforeseen costs, such as medical emergencies or car repairs, without debt. Having a financial cushion helps alleviate restlessness associated with financial uncertainty.

Seek Professional Help:

If you find yourself overwhelmed or uncertain about your financial situation, don't hesitate to seek the assistance of a financial advisor or counselor.

These professionals can provide guidance, develop a personalized financial plan, and offer insights to address specific financial concerns. Consulting experts can help you gain confidence in managing your finances and reduce restlessness.

Remember, managing your money is a continuous journey, not a fixed destination. Financial restlessness is a shared experience, and it's essential to acknowledge it as a normal part of the financial landscape. By taking small, consistent steps and making informed financial decisions, you can alleviate restlessness, gain control over your finances, and work toward your financial goals.

In essence, financial restlessness can be managed by adopting practical financial strategies, setting clear intentions, and building a solid financial foundation. By doing so, you can navigate the ups and downs of your financial journey with greater confidence and peace of mind.

In this context, understanding the psychology behind boredom spending is crucial. The pleasure derived from acquiring new possessions or indulging in temporary experiences can be enticing. However, it often leads to financial regret once the initial excitement disappears.

4

Chapter 4: Uncovering the Hidden Masks and Camouflage of Financial Deceit

In the world of finance, transparency is a fundamental cornerstone of trust and ethical conduct. However, the practice of masking or concealing one's true financial situation is a common yet damaging behavior. This chapter explores the complex reasons behind these financial masks and emphasizes the importance of embracing financial transparency.

The Damage of Financial Deception

Erosion of Trust:
Lack of financial transparency can cause profound damage to trust. Whether within personal relationships or in business dealings, keeping financial secrets can undermine the foundation of trust essential for collaboration and cooperation. People may start to question your honesty and integrity, not just in financial matters but in all aspects of your life.

Impaired Decision-Making:
The secrecy surrounding financial matters, whether self-deception or withholding information from a significant other like your spouse, can have far-reaching consequences, extending beyond mere decision-making into the relationship dynamics. By not providing a complete and honest account of your financial situation, the choices you make are subject to being based on distorted or incomplete information.

Consider the scenario where one might conceal the extent of their debts from themselves or their partner. This lack of transparency can lead to ill-informed decisions, such as taking on loans that exceed their realistic ability to repay. Similarly, investing in ventures with high-risk profiles without a comprehensive understanding of potential repercussions becomes more likely when financial truths are hidden.

The repercussions of these choices extend beyond immediate financial strain. A lack of clarity in financial communication can set the stage for a gradual depletion of wealth and stability. The strain caused by accumulating debt or unforeseen losses can strain relationships, trust and cause emotional turmoil.

Furthermore, the absence of open and honest conversations about finances can hinder the establishment shared financial goals and plans. This lack of alignment in financial objectives may sow the seeds of discord and resentment, as partners may find themselves working towards conflicting aspirations.

In essence, the act of concealing financial truths has a dual impact. It compromises the quality of financial decision-making and jeopardizes the foundation of trust and understanding in relationships.

Transparency and open communication about financial matters is essential to fostering a healthy financial environment and maintaining strong interpersonal connections.

Barriers to Getting Help:

Financial struggles can affect anyone, and it's natural to seek assistance when facing difficulties. However, when you conceal your financial challenges, you create barriers that prevent others from offering support. Whether seeking advice from a financial expert, borrowing money from a friend or family member, or participating in a debt management program, transparency about your financial situation is the first step toward getting the help you need.

Potential Legal Consequences:

The consequences of financial deception can extend to the legal sphere, depending on the severity of the situation. Engaging in fraudulent activities to conceal assets, income, or liabilities can lead to legal trouble. For instance, in bankruptcy cases, failing to disclose assets can lead to criminal penalties. Recognizing that the law values transparency in financial matters is essential, and concealing the truth can have severe legal repercussions.

The Power of Financial Transparency
Financial transparency is not just a matter of ethics but also a strategic choice leading to better financial outcomes. Here's how embracing financial transparency can benefit you:

Strengthened Trust:
By being honest and transparent about your financial situation, you build trust with yourself and others, both personally and professionally. Transparent financial dealings are the foundation of successful partnerships and collaborations.
Trust is vital whether you're working with business partners, seeking investments, or managing personal finances as a couple.

Informed Decision-Making:
Transparent financial information empowers you to make informed and rational decisions. When you clearly understand your financial position, you can set realistic goals, create an effective financial plan, and distribute resources appropriately. Informed decisions lead to

financial stability and growth.

Access to Assistance:
Being open about your financial challenges allows you to access the assistance you may need.

Financial advisors, debt counselors, and even friends and family can provide valuable guidance and support when they understand your financial situation. You are more likely to receive help when you are candid about your needs.

Avoidance of Legal Trouble:
Maintaining financial transparency helps you stay on the right side of the law. You can avoid the legal complications and potential penalties associated with financial deception. Honesty and compliance with legal and financial regulations are essential for a trouble-free financial life.

Embracing financial transparency is a step toward financial well-being.

In conclusion, financial transparency is not just a moral imperative; it is a strategic choice that can improve your financial outcomes and protect you from legal complications. By shedding the masks of financial deception and embracing openness in financial dealings, you can build trust, make informed decisions, access assistance when needed, and confidently navigate the complexities of your financial life.

5

Chapter 5: Getting to the Roots of Trust and Confidence while Navigating Financial Challenges

Trust and confidence are essential components of a healthy financial relationship. However, issues related to trust and self-confidence can significantly impact financial decisions and behaviors. In this chapter, we will explore the trust and confidence issues that individuals often face in their financial lives and discuss strategies to overcome these barriers.

Trust Issues Concerning Money

Trust issues concerning money can manifest in various forms, affecting individuals' ability to save, invest, or even care about their financial well-being. These issues can be complex and deeply rooted in an individual's experiences and beliefs. Here are some common reasons behind trust issues related to money:

Past Experiences with Financial Institutions:

Negative interactions with banks, investment firms, or financial advisors in the past can erode trust. A dispute, an investment that underperformed, or unethical practices can lead to skepticism about entrusting one's money to financial institutions.

Cultural Background:

Discussing money, investments, or financial matters in certain cultures is considered taboo. This cultural hostility to financial discussions can lead to a lack of trust in the financial system and can hinder financial literacy.

Lack of Knowledge:

Many individuals lack a solid understanding of personal finance and investing. This lack of knowledge can result in a lack of trust in the financial process, as they may feel overwhelmed by the complexity of financial decisions.

Fear of Losing Money:
The fear of losing money is a common barrier to trust when it comes to investing. People may fear that they don't fully understand the risks involved or could lose their hard-earned money. This fear can paralyze them and prevent them from taking necessary steps to secure their financial future.

Lack of Financial Stability:
For individuals who are struggling financially, the idea of saving may seem out of reach. The perception that they cannot afford to save can aggravate their trust issues concerning money.

Overcoming trust issues concerning money is not always easy, but it is essential for financial well-being. Seeking help from a financial advisor or engaging in personal financial education can be pivotal in rebuilding trust in the financial system. It's important to remember that trust can be repaired over time with the proper knowledge and support, ultimately leading to a healthier financial relationship.

Confidence Issues

Confidence, or the lack thereof, can significantly influence financial decisions and actions. A lack of confidence in one's financial abilities can lead to various excuses and behaviors that hinder financial stability. Let's explore some of the common financial excuses that may stem from confidence issues and discuss ways to overcome them:

"I'm Not Good with Numbers":

Many individuals avoid financial management because they believe they lack the necessary numerical skills. However, managing personal finances doesn't require advanced mathematical abilities. Basic financial literacy can be acquired by taking small steps, such as creating a budget and tracking expenses.

"I Don't Deserve to Be Wealthy":

This limiting belief can prevent individuals from taking actions that lead to financial success. It's important to recognize that financial well-being is not a measure of an individual's worth. Everyone has the potential to achieve financial stability and success.

Overcoming confidence issues is a journey that may take time and effort, but it is a crucial step toward achieving financial stability. Here are some strategies to build confidence in your financial decision-making:

Education and Self-Improvement:
Invest in your financial education. There are numerous resources, courses, and books available to help you enhance your financial literacy. Knowledge is a powerful tool to boost your confidence.

Start Small:
Begin with manageable financial goals and tasks. As you achieve these smaller goals, your confidence will naturally grow, paving the way for more substantial financial accomplishments.

Seek Guidance:
Don't hesitate to seek advice from financial professionals or mentors. They can provide valuable insights and guidance to help you make informed financial decisions.

Challenge Limiting Beliefs:
Recognize and challenge limiting beliefs that hinder your financial progress. Replace negative thoughts with positive affirmations and constructive self-talk.

Track Progress:
Regularly track your financial progress and celebrate your achievements. These milestones can boost your confidence and motivation to continue on your financial journey.

In conclusion, trust and confidence are essential to financial well-being. Overcoming trust issues concerning money and building confidence in your financial abilities is a journey that can lead to greater financial stability, improved decision-making, and a healthier relationship with money. By addressing these issues, individuals can take control of their financial future and work towards their financial goals with greater assurance.

6

Chapter 6: Correcting Misconceptions About Money

Money is a subject that often carries with it a host of misconceptions and misunderstandings. These misconceptions can significantly influence people's financial behaviors and attitudes. In this chapter, we will explore some common misconceptions about money and discuss why correcting these misunderstandings is essential.

Misconceptions About Money:

Money is the Key to Happiness:

It's a widely held belief that money is the key to happiness. While financial stability can make life more comfortable, happiness is a complex and multifaceted emotion that cannot be purchased. True happiness comes from within, from experiences, relationships, and personal fulfillment. No amount of money can replace the joy that comes from authentic connections and self-fulfillment.

More Money Means Less Stress:

While having more money can eliminate specific financial stressors, it can also introduce new ones. People with greater wealth may worry about losing it, managing their assets, or discerning true friends from those interested in their wealth. Financial success doesn't automatically eliminate stress; it merely shifts the nature of the stressors.

Money is the Root of All Evil:

This is a common misquotation of a biblical verse stating, "The love of money is the root of all kinds of evil." Money itself is not inherently evil; it's a tool, a medium of exchange. However, when people become excessively focused on accumulating wealth at any cost, it can lead to unethical actions and moral compromises. Money is a neutral entity; it's the intentions and values of individuals that determine its impact.

You Have to Be Born Into Wealth to Be Rich:

It's a misconception that being born into a wealthy family is a prerequisite for accumulating wealth.

While inherited wealth can undoubtedly provide a head start, many self-made millionaires and billionaires started with limited resources and built their fortunes through hard work, innovation, and perseverance. The journey to financial success is open to anyone willing to put in the effort.

Money Can Solve All Your Problems:
While money can be a powerful tool for addressing financial challenges, it cannot solve all of life's problems. Health issues, relationship conflicts, personal struggles, and emotional well-being are not problems that can be resolved solely through financial means.

A holistic approach is necessary to address these aspects of life.

The Importance of Correcting Misconceptions:

Correcting misconceptions about money is vital for fostering a healthy relationship with finances. Misunderstandings can lead to unrealistic expectations, unhealthy attitudes, and potentially harmful financial decisions. By recognizing and addressing these misconceptions, individuals can develop a more balanced and realistic perspective on money.

In conclusion, the journey to financial wellness involves practical financial strategies and emotional and psychological well-being.

Correcting misconceptions about money is a fundamental step toward achieving a balanced and empowered relationship with finances. By understanding that money is a tool, not a source of happiness, and acknowledging its limitations, individuals can pursue a path that leads to financial stability, personal fulfillment, and overall well-being.

Conclusion of the Book - "What's Really Behind the Excuses"

In this book, we took a dive into the complexities of financial behaviors and the excuses that often underlie them. We've explored the emotional and psychological factors influencing how individuals approach their finances, make decisions, and form attitudes toward money. The journey of self-discovery in the context of personal finance is profound and can be transformative.

Financial excuses are more than surface-level justifications for behaviors; they are often rooted in deep-seated emotions, beliefs, and experiences. Acknowledging and addressing these excuses is the first step toward a healthier, more empowered relationship with money. It's about recognizing that financial wellness encompasses practical strategies, emotional well-being, and self-awareness.

At the conclusion of this book, we reiterate the importance of recognizing and addressing the underlying emotional factors that influence clients' financial behaviors. We emphasize that true financial wellness goes beyond mere numbers; it involves a holistic approach that integrates emotional well-being with practical financial strategies. By acknowledging their excuses and embracing the journey of self-discovery, clients can move toward a more empowered and fulfilling relationship with their finances.

The journey to financial wellness is ongoing and unique to each individual. It involves facing one's fears, confronting limiting beliefs, and making intentional choices. It's about understanding that financial decisions are not purely rational but are deeply intertwined with emotions, experiences, and personal values.

As we conclude this book, we encourage readers to embark on their own journey of self-discovery and financial empowerment. By doing so, individuals can break free from the constraints of excuses, achieve greater financial stability, and lead more fulfilled lives. Financial wellness is not just about money; it's about the freedom and peace of mind that come from understanding and embracing the factors driving financial behaviors.

In closing, we invite readers to take the insights and lessons from this book and apply them to their financial lives. The path to financial wellness may be challenging but worth taking. By addressing the excuses, understanding the emotions, and making intentional choices, individuals can chart a course toward a brighter and more secure financial future.

MEET THE AUTHOR

Meet Kim, a seasoned professional in financial education with a rich background in coordinating classes, workshops, and impactful speaking engagements. Her expertise shines in her signature presentation, "Getting to the Root of the Matter."

As the founder of Nickels & Dimes Solutions L.L.C., Kim joyfully imparts her wisdom. Beyond her financial acumen, she's a dedicated mother of two and a proud grandmother of six, fueled by a passion for empowering others.

Kim's influence extends to SHIFT TV, where she shares her financial insights. Alongside her coaching, she's a prolific author of three impactful books, all available on Amazon: "Restart - A Journey to Becoming Debt-Free," "Rediscover Your Voice," and "Always Mom."

Discover Kim's transformative guidance and wealth of knowledge as she continues to inspire and empower through her diverse contributions in the financial realm.

@nickelsandimesolutions.com